THE AESTHETIC
DIMENSION

OTHER WORKS BY AND ABOUT
HERBERT MARCUSE
PUBLISHED BY BEACON PRESS

Counterrevolution and Revolt, by Herbert Marcuse (1972)

The Critical Spirit: Essays in Honor of Herbert Marcuse,
edited by Kurt H. Wolff and Barrington Moore, Jr.
(1967)

A Critique of Pure Tolerance, by Robert Paul Wolff,
Barrington Moore, Jr., and Herbert Marcuse (1965)

Eros and Civilization: A Philosophical Inquiry into Freud,
by Herbert Marcuse (1955, 1966)

An Essay on Liberation, by Herbert Marcuse (1966)

Five Lectures: Psychoanalysis, Politics, and Utopia, by
Herbert Marcuse (1970)

Negations: Essays in Critical Theory, by Herbert Marcuse
(1968)

*One-Dimensional Man: Studies in the Ideology of
Advanced Industrial Society,* by Herbert Marcuse
(1964)

*Reason and Revolution: Hegel and the Rise of Social
Theory,* by Herbert Marcuse (1960)

Studies in Critical Philosophy, by Herbert Marcuse (1973)

THE AESTHETIC
DIMENSION

TOWARD A CRITIQUE OF
MARXIST AESTHETICS

HERBERT
MARCUSE

Beacon Press   Boston

Originally published in German under the title *Die Permanenz der Kunst: Wider eine bestimmte Marxistische Aesthetik* (Munich: Carl Hanser Verlag, copyright © 1977 by Herbert Marcuse)

English version translated and revised by Herbert Marcuse and Erica Sherover, copyright © 1978

Beacon Press books are published under the auspices of the Unitarian Universalist Association

Published simultaneously in Canada by Fitzhenry & Whiteside Limited, Toronto

Printed in the United States of America

(hardcover) 9 8 7 6 5 4 3 2 1

Library of Congress Cataloging in Publication Data

Marcuse, Herbert, 1896–

    The aesthetic dimension.
    Translation of Die Permanenz der Kunst.
    Bibliography: p.
    Includes index.
    1. Marx, Karl, 1818–1883 — Aesthetics — Addresses, essays, lectures.   1. Title.
B3305.M74M3513   1978   335.4'11   76–9001
ISBN 0–8070–1518–0

Contents

Acknowledgments

Erica Sherover has given the manuscript a critical reading from the first draft to the final version. She has discussed with me every paragraph, and insisted on improvements. This little book is dedicated to her: my wife, friend, and collaborator.

Intensive discussions with my friends Leo Lowenthal and Reinhard Lettau have been a great help and a great pleasure. Leo Lowenthal has again proved his reputation as a fierce reader and critic; Reinhard Lettau has demonstrated that authentic literature—literature as resistance—is still possible today.

My stepsons Osha and Michael Neumann gave me stimulating suggestions: Michael by his encouraging comments, Osha in lively conversations about his own work in art.

My son Peter, whose work in urban planning led us to common problems, has again been a dear friend and advisor.

I am particularly grateful to Catherine Asmann who typed about half a dozen versions of this essay—and liked it.

My debt to the aesthetic theory of Theodor W. Adorno does not require any specific acknowledgment.

Preface

This essay seeks to contribute to Marxist aesthetics through questioning its predominant orthodoxy. By "orthodoxy" I understand the interpretation of the quality and truth of a work of art in terms of the totality of the prevailing relations of production. Specifically, this interpretation holds that the work of art represents the interests and world outlook of particular social classes in a more or less accurate manner.

My critique of this orthodoxy is grounded in Marxist theory inasmuch as it also views art in the context of the prevailing social relations, and ascribes to art a political function and a political potential. But in contrast to orthodox Marxist aesthetics I see the political potential of art in art itself, in the aesthetic form as such. Furthermore, I argue that by virtue of its aesthetic form, art is largely autonomous vis à vis the given social relations. In its autonomy art both protests these relations, and at the same time transcends them. Thereby art subverts the dominant consciousness, the ordinary experience.

Some preliminary remarks: although this essay speaks of "art" in general, my discussion is essentially focused on literature, primarily the literature of the eighteenth and nineteenth centuries.

I do not feel qualified to talk about music and the visual arts, though I believe that what holds true for literature, *mutatis mutandis,* may also apply to these arts. Secondly, in reference to the selection of the works discussed, the objection that I operate with a self-validating hypothesis seems justified. I term those works "authentic" or "great" which fulfill aesthetic criteria previously defined as constitutive of "authentic" or "great" art. In defense, I would say that throughout the long history of art, and in spite of changes in taste, there is a standard which remains constant. This standard not only allows us to distinguish between "high" and "trivial" literature, opera and operetta, comedy and slapstick, but also between good and bad art within these genres. There is a demonstrable qualitative difference between Shakespeare's comedies and the Restoration Comedy, between Goethe's and Schiller's poems, between Balzac's *Comédie humaine* and Zola's *Rougon-Macquart.*

Art can be called revolutionary in several senses. In a narrow sense, art may be revolutionary if it represents a radical change in style and technique. Such change may be the achievement of a genuine avant-garde, anticipating or reflecting substantial changes in the society at large. Thus, expressionism and surrealism anticipated the destructiveness of monopoly capitalism, and the emergence of new goals of radical change. But the merely "technical" definition of revolutionary art says nothing about the quality of the work, nothing about its authenticity and truth.

Beyond this, a work of art can be called revolutionary if, by virtue of the aesthetic transformation, it represents, in the exemplary fate of individuals, the prevailing unfreedom and the rebelling forces, thus breaking through the mystified (and petrified) social reality, and opening the horizon of change (liberation).

In this sense, every authentic work of art would be revolutionary, i.e., subversive of perception and understanding, an indictment of the established reality, the appearance of the image of liberation. This would hold true of the classical drama as well as Brecht's plays, of Goethe's *Wahlverwandtschaften* as well as Günter Grass's *Hundejahre*, of William Blake as well as Rimbaud.

The obvious difference in the representation of the subversive potential is due to the difference in social structure with which these works are confronted: the distribution of oppression among the population, the composition and function of the ruling class, the given possibilities of radical change. These historical conditions are present in the work in several ways: explicitly, or as background and horizon, and in the language and imagery. But they are the specific historical expressions and manifestations of the same transhistorical substance of art: its own dimension of truth, protest and promise, a dimension constituted by the aesthetic form. Thus, Büchner's *Woyzeck,* Brecht's plays, but also Kafka's and Beckett's novels and stories are revolutionary by virtue of the form given to the content. Indeed the content (the established reality) appears in these works only as estranged and mediated. The truth of art lies in this: that the world really is as it appears in the work of art.

This thesis implies that literature is not revolutionary because it is written for the working class or for "the revolution." Literature can be called revolutionary in a meaningful sense only with reference to itself, as content having become form. The political potential of art lies only in its own aesthetic dimension. Its relation to praxis is inexorably indirect, mediated, and frustrating. The more immediately political the work of art, the more it reduces the power of estrangement and the radical, transcendent goals of change. In this sense, there may be more subversive potential in the poetry of Baudelaire and Rimbaud than in the didactic plays of Brecht.

THE AESTHETIC
DIMENSION

In a situation where the miserable reality can be changed only through radical political praxis, the concern with aesthetics demands justification. It would be senseless to deny the element of despair inherent in this concern: the retreat into a world of fiction where existing conditions are changed and overcome only in the realm of the imagination. However, this purely ideological conception of art is being questioned with increasing intensity. It seems that art as art expresses a truth, an experience, a necessity which, although not in the domain of radical praxis, are nevertheless essential components of revolution. With this insight, the basic conception of Marxist aesthetics, that is its treatment of art as ideology, and the emphasis on the class character of art, become again the topic of critical reexamination.[1]

This discussion is directed to the following theses of Marxist aesthetics:

1. There is a definite connection between art and the material base, between art and the totality of the relations of production. With the change in production relations, art itself is transformed as part of the superstructure, although, like other ideologies, it can lag behind or anticipate social change.

2. There is a definite connection between art and social class. The only authentic, true, progressive art is the art of an ascending class. It expresses the consciousness of this class.

3. Consequently, the political and the aesthetic, the revolutionary content and the artistic quality tend to coincide.

4. The writer has an obligation to articulate and express the interests and needs of the ascending class. (In capitalism, this would be the proletariat.)

5. A declining class or its representatives are unable to produce anything but "decadent" art.

6. Realism (in various senses) is considered as the art form which corresponds most adequately to the social relationships, and thus is the "correct" art form.

Each of these theses implies that the social relations of production must be represented in the literary work—not imposed upon the work externally, but a part of its inner logic and the logic of the material.

This aesthetic imperative follows from the base-superstructure conception. In contrast to the rather dialectical formulations of Marx and Engels, the conception has been made into a rigid schema, a schematization that has had devastating consequences for aesthetics. The schema implies a normative notion of the material base as the true reality and a political devaluation of nonmaterial forces particularly of the individual consciousness and subconscious and their political function. This function can be either regressive or emancipatory. In both cases, it can become a material force. If historical materialism does not account for this role of subjectivity, it takes on the coloring of vulgar materialism.

Ideology becomes mere ideology, in spite of Engels's emphatic qualifications, and a devaluation of the entire realm of subjectivity takes place, a devaluation not only of the subject as *ego cogito,* the rational subject, but also of inwardness, emotions, and imagination. The subjectivity of individuals, their own consciousness and unconscious tends to be dissolved into class consciousness. Thereby, a major prerequisite of revolution is minimized, namely, the fact that the need for radical change must be rooted in the subjectivity of individuals themselves, in their intelligence and their passions, their drives and their goals. Marxist theory succumbed to that very reification which it had exposed and combated in society as a whole. Subjectivity became an atom of objectivity; even in its rebellious form it was surrendered to a collective consciousness. The deterministic component of Marxist theory does not lie in its concept of the relationship between social existence and consciousness, but in the reductionistic concept of consciousness which brackets the particular content of individual consciousness and, with it, the subjective potential for revolution.

This development was furthered by the interpretation of subjectivity as a "bourgeois" notion. Historically, this is questionable.[2] But even in bourgeois society, insistence on the truth and right of inwardness is not really a bourgeois value. With the affirmation of the inwardness of subjectivity, the individual steps out of the network of exchange relationships and exchange values, withdraws from the reality of bourgeois society, and enters another dimension of existence. Indeed, this escape from reality led to an experience which could (and did) become a powerful force in *invalidating* the actually prevailing bourgeois values, namely, by shifting the locus of the individual's realization from the domain of the performance principle and the profit motive to that of the inner resources of the human being: passion, imagination, conscience. Moreover, withdrawal and retreat were not the last position. Subjectivity strove to break out of its inwardness into the material and intellectual culture. And today, in the totalitarian period, it has become a political value as a counter-force against aggressive and exploitative social-ization.

Liberating subjectivity constitutes itself in the inner history of the individuals—their own history, which is not identical with their social existence. It is the particular history of their encounters, their passions, joys, and sorrows—experiences which are not necessarily grounded in their class situation, and which are not even comprehensible from this perspective. To be sure, the actual manifestations of their history are determined by their class situation, but this situation is not the ground of their fate—of that which happens to them. Especially in its nonmaterial aspects it explodes the class framework. It is all too easy to relegate love and hate, joy and sorrow, hope and despair to the domain of psychology, thereby removing them from the concerns of radical praxis.

Indeed, in terms of political economy they may not be "forces of production," but for every human being they are decisive, they constitute reality. Even in its most distinguished representatives Marxist aesthetics has shared in the devaluation of subjectivity. Hence the preference for realism as the model of progressive art; the denigration of romanticism as simply reactionary; the denunciation of "decadent" art—in general, the embarrassment when confronted with the task of evaluating the aesthetic qualities of a work in terms other than class ideologies.

I shall submit the following thesis: the radical qualities of art, that is to say, its indictment of the established reality and its invocation of the beautiful image (*schöner Schein*) of liberation are grounded precisely in the dimensions where art *transcends* its social determination and emancipates itself from the given universe of discourse and behavior while preserving its overwhelming presence. Thereby art creates the realm in which the subversion of experience proper to art becomes possible: the world formed by art is recognized as a reality which is suppressed and distorted in the given reality. This experience culminates in extreme situations (of love and death, guilt and failure, but also joy, happiness, and fulfillment) which explode the given reality in the name of a truth normally denied or even unheard. The inner logic of the work of art terminates in the emergence of another reason, another sensibility, which defy the rationality and sensibility incorporated in the dominant social institutions.

Under the law of the aesthetic form, the given reality is necessarily *sublimated:* the immediate content is stylized, the "data" are reshaped and reordered in accordance with the demands of the art form, which requires that even the representation of death and destruction invoke the need for hope—a need rooted in the new consciousness embodied in the work of art.

Aesthetic sublimation makes for the affirmative, reconciling component of art,[3] though it is at the same time a vehicle for the critical, negating function of art. The transcendence of immediate reality shatters the reified objectivity of established social relations and opens a new dimension of experience: rebirth of the rebellious subjectivity. Thus, on the basis of aesthetic sublimation, a *desublimation* takes place in the perception of individuals—in their feelings, judgments, thoughts; an invalidation of dominant norms, needs, and values. With all its affirmative-ideological features, art remains a dissenting force.

We can tentatively define "aesthetic form" as the result of the transformation of a given content (actual or historical, personal or social fact) into a self-contained whole: a poem, play, novel, etc.[4] The work is thus "taken out" of the constant process of reality and assumes a significance and truth of its own. The aesthetic transformation is achieved through a reshaping of language, perception, and understanding so that they reveal the essence of reality in its appearance: the repressed potentialities of man and nature. The work of art thus re-presents reality while accusing it.[5]

The critical function of art, its contribution to the struggle for liberation, resides in the aesthetic form. A work of art is authentic or true not by virtue of its content (i.e., the "correct" representation of social conditions), nor by its "pure" form, but by the content having become form.

True, the aesthetic form removes art from the actuality of the class struggle—from actuality pure and simple. The aesthetic form constitutes the autonomy of art vis à vis "the given." However, this dissociation does not produce "false consciousness" or mere illusion but rather a counter-consciousness: negation of the realistic-conformist mind.

Aesthetic form, autonomy, and truth are interrelated. Each is a socio-historical phenomenon, and each *transcends* the socio-historical arena. While the latter limits the autonomy of art it does so without invalidating the *trans*historical truths expressed in the work. The truth of art lies in its power to break the monopoly of established reality (i.e., of those who established it) to *define* what is *real*. In this rupture, which is the achievement of the aesthetic form, the fictitious world of art appears as true reality.

Art is committed to that perception of the world which alienates individuals from their functional existence and performance in society— it is committed to an emancipation of sensibility, imagination, and reason in all spheres of subjectivity and objectivity. The aesthetic transformation becomes a vehicle of recognition and indictment. But this achievement presupposes a degree of autonomy which withdraws art from the mystifying power of the given and frees it for the expression of its own truth. Inasmuch as man and nature are constituted by an unfree society, their repressed and distorted potentialities can be represented only in an *estranging* form. The world of art is that of another *Reality Principle,* of estrangement—and only as estrangement does art fulfill a *cognitive* function: it communicates truths not communicable in any other language; *it contradicts.*

However, the strong affirmative tendencies toward reconciliation with the established reality coexist with the rebellious ones. I shall try to show that they are not due to the specific class determination of art but rather to the redeeming character of the *catharsis.* The catharsis itself is grounded in the power of aesthetic form to call fate by its name, to demystify its force, to give the word to the victims—the power of recognition which gives the individual a modicum of freedom and fulfillment in the realm of unfreedom. The interplay between the affirmation and the indictment of that which is, between ideology and truth, pertains to the very structure of art.[6] But in the authentic works, the affirmation does not cancel the indictment: reconciliation and hope still preserve the memory of things past.

The affirmative character of art has yet another source: it is in the commitment of art to

Eros, the deep affirmation of the Life Instincts in their fight against instinctual and social oppression. The permanence of art, its historical immortality throughout the millenia of destruction, bears witness to this commitment.

Art stands under the law of the given, while transgressing this law. The concept of art as an essentially autonomous and negating productive force contradicts the notion which sees art as performing an essentially dependent, affirmative-ideological function, that is to say, glorifying and absolving the existing society.[7] Even the militant bourgeois literature of the eighteenth century remains ideological: the struggle of the ascending class with the nobility is primarily over issues of bourgeois morality. The lower classes play only a marginal role, if any. With a few notable exceptions, this literature is not one of class struggle. According to this point of view, the ideological character of art can be remedied today only by grounding art in revolutionary praxis and in the *Weltanschauung* of the proletariat.

It has often been pointed out that this interpretation of art does not do justice to the views of Marx and Engels.[8] To be sure, even this interpretation admits that art aims at representing the essence of a given reality and not merely its appearance. Reality is taken to be the totality of social relations and its essence is defined as the laws determining these relations in the "complex of social causality." [9] This view demands that the protagonists in a work of art represent individuals as "types" who in turn exemplify "objective tendencies of social development, indeed of humanity as a whole." [10]

Such formulations provoke the question whether literature is not hereby assigned a function which could only be fulfilled in the medium of theory. The representation of the social totality requires a conceptual analysis, which can hardly be transposed into the medium of sensibility. During the great debate on Marxist aesthetics in the early thirties, Lu Märten suggested that Marxist theory possesses a theoretical form of its own which militates against any attempt to give it an aesthetic form.[11]

But if the work of art cannot be comprehended in terms of social theory, neither can it be comprehended in terms of philosophy. In his discussion with Adorno, Lucien Goldmann rejects Adorno's claim that in order to understand a literary work "one has to transcend it towards philosophy, philosophical culture and critical knowledge." Against Adorno, Goldmann insists on the concreteness immanent in the work which makes it into an (aesthetic) totality in its own right: "The work of art is a universe of colors, sounds and words, and concrete characters. There is no death, there is only Phaedra dying." [12]

The reification of Marxist aesthetics depreciates and distorts the truth expressed in this universe —it minimizes the cognitive function of art as ideology. For the radical potential of art lies precisely in its ideological character, in its transcendent relation to the "basis." Ideology is not always *mere* ideology, false consciousness. The consciousness and the representation of truths which appear as abstract in relation to the established process of production are also ideological functions. Art presents one of these truths. As ideology, it opposes the given society. The autonomy of art contains the categorical imperative: "things must change." If the liberation of human beings and nature is to be possible at all, then the social nexus of destruction and submission must be broken. This does not mean that the revolution becomes thematic; on the contrary, in the aesthetically most perfect works, it does not. It seems that in these works the

necessity of revolution is presupposed, as the
a priori of art. But the revolution is also as it were
surpassed and questioned as to how far it re-
sponds to the anguish of the human being, as to
how far it achieves a rupture with the past.

Compared with the often one-dimensional
optimism of propaganda, art is permeated with
pessimism, not seldom intertwined with comedy.
Its "liberating laughter" recalls the danger and the
evil that have passed—this time! But the pessimism
of art is not counterrevolutionary. It serves to
warn against the "happy consciousness" of radical
praxis: as if all of that which art invokes and in-
dicts could be settled through the class struggle.
Such pessimism permeates even the literature in
which the revolution itself is affirmed, and becomes
thematic; Büchner's play, *The Death of Danton*
is a classic example.

Marxist aesthetics assumes that all art is
somehow conditioned by the relations of production,
class position, and so on. Its first task (but only
its first) is the specific analysis of this "somehow,"
that is to say, of the limits and modes of this
conditioning. The question as to whether there are
qualities of art which transcend specific social

conditions and how these qualities are related to the particular social conditions remains open. Marxist aesthetics has yet to ask: What are the qualities of art which transcend the specific social content and form and give art its universality? Marxist aesthetics must explain why Greek tragedy and the medieval epic, for example, can still be experienced today as "great," "authentic" literature, even though they pertain to ancient slave society and feudalism respectively. Marx's remark at the end of *The Introduction to the Critique of Political Economy* is hardly persuasive; one simply cannot explain the attraction of Greek art for us today as our rejoicing in the unfolding of the social "childhood of humanity."

However correctly one has analyzed a poem, play, or novel in terms of its social content, the questions as to whether the particular work is good, beautiful, and true are still unanswered. But the answers to these questions cannot again be given in terms of the specific relations of production which constitute the historical context of the respective work. The circularity of this method is obvious. In addition it falls victim to an easy relativism which is contradicted clearly enough by the permanence of certain qualities of art through all changes of style and historical periods (transcendence, estrangement, aesthetic order, manifestations of the beautiful).

The fact that a work truly represents the interests or the outlook of the proletariat or of the bourgeoisie does not yet make it an authentic work of art. This "material" quality may facilitate its reception, may lend it greater concreteness, but it is in no way constitutive. The universality of art cannot be grounded in the world and world outlook of a particular class, for art envisions a concrete universal, humanity (*Menschlichkeit*), which no particular class can incorporate, not even the proletariat, Marx's "universal class." The inexorable entanglement of joy and sorrow, celebration and despair, Eros and Thanatos cannot be dissolved into problems of class struggle. History is also grounded in nature. And Marxist theory has the least justification to ignore the metabolism between the human being and nature, and to denounce the insistence on this natural soil of society as a regressive ideological conception.

The emergence of human beings as "species beings"—men and women capable of living in that community of freedom which is the potential of the species—this is the subjective basis of a classless society. Its realization presupposes a radical transformation of the drives and needs of the individuals: an organic development within the socio-historical. Solidarity would be on weak grounds were it not rooted in the instinctual structure of individuals. In this dimension, men and women are confronted with psycho-physical forces which they have to make their own without being able to overcome the naturalness of these forces. This is the domain of the primary drives: of libidinal and destructive energy. Solidarity and community have their basis in the subordination of destructive and aggressive energy to the social emancipation of the life instincts.

Marxism has too long neglected the radical political potential of this dimension, though the revolutionizing of the instinctual structure is a prerequisite for a change in the system of needs, the mark of a socialist society as qualitative difference. Class society knows only the appearance, the image of the qualitative difference; this image, divorced from praxis, has been preserved in the realm of art. In the aesthetic form, the autonomy of art constitutes itself. It was forced upon art through the separation of mental and material labor, as a result of the prevailing relations of domination. Dissociation from the process of production became a refuge and a vantage point from which to denounce the reality established through domination.

Nevertheless society remains present in the autonomous realm of art in several ways: first of all as the "stuff" for the aesthetic representation which, past and present, is transformed in this representation. This is the historicity of the conceptual, linguistic, and imaginable material which the tradition transmits to the artists and with or against which they have to work; secondly, as the scope of the actually available possibilities of struggle and liberation; thirdly as the specific position of art in the social division of labor, especially in the separation of intellectual and manual labor through which artistic activity, and to a great extent also its reception, become the privilege of an "elite" removed from the material process of production.

The class character of art consists only in these objective limitations of its autonomy. The fact that the artist belongs to a privileged group negates neither the truth nor the aesthetic quality of his work. What is true of "the classics of socialism" is true also of the great artists: they break through the class limitations of their family, background, environment. Marxist theory is not family research. The progressive character of art, its contribution to the struggle for liberation cannot be measured by the artists' origins nor by the ideological horizon of their class. Neither can it be determined by the presence (or absence) of the oppressed class in their works. The criteria for the progressive character of art are given only in the work itself as a whole: in what it says and how it says it.

In this sense art is "art for art's sake" inasmuch as the aesthetic form reveals tabooed and repressed dimensions of reality: aspects of liberation. The poetry of Mallarmé is an extreme example; his poems conjure up modes of perception, imagination, gestures—a feast of sensuousness which shatters everyday experience and anticipates a different reality principle.

The degree to which the distance and estrangement from praxis constitute the emancipatory value of art becomes particularly clear in those works of literature which seem to close themselves rigidly against such praxis. Walter Benjamin has traced this in the works of Poe, Baudelaire, Proust, and Valéry. They express a "consciousness of crisis" (*Krisenbewusstsein*): a pleasure in decay, in destruction, in the beauty of evil; a celebration of the asocial, of the anomic—the secret rebellion of the bourgeois against his own class. Benjamin writes about Baudelaire:

> It seems of little value to give his work a position on the most advanced ramparts of the human struggle for liberation. From the beginning, it appears much more promising to follow him in his machinations where he is without doubt at home: in the enemy camp. These machinations are a blessing for the enemy only in the rarest cases. Baudelaire was a secret agent, an agent of the secret discontent of his class with its own rule. One who confronts Baudelaire with this class gets more out of him than one who rejects him as uninteresting from a proletarian standpoint.[13]

The "secret" protest of this esoteric literature lies in the ingression of the primary erotic-destructive forces which explode the normal universe of communication and behavior. They are asocial in their very nature, a subterranean rebellion against the social order. Inasmuch as this literature reveals the dominion of Eros and Thanatos beyond all social control, it invokes needs and gratifications which are essentially destructive. In terms of political praxis, this literature remains elitist and decadent. It does nothing in the struggle for liberation—except to open the tabooed zones of nature and society in which even death and the devil are enlisted as allies in the refusal to abide by the law and order of repression. This literature is one of the historical forms of critical aesthetic transcendence. Art cannot abolish the social division of labor which makes for its esoteric character, but neither can art "popularize" itself without weakening its emancipatory impact.

Art's separation from the process of material production has enabled it to demystify the reality reproduced in this process. Art challenges the monopoly of the established reality to determine what is "real," and it does so by creating a fictitious world which is nevertheless "more real than reality itself." [14]

To ascribe the nonconformist, autonomous qualities of art to aesthetic form is to place them outside "engaged literature," outside the realm of praxis and production. Art has its own language and illuminates reality only through this other language. Moreover art has its own dimension of affirmation and negation, a dimension which cannot be coordinated with the social process of production.

To be sure, it is possible to transfer the action of *Hamlet* or *Iphigenia* from the courtly world of the upper classes into the world of material production; one can also change the historical framework and modernize the plot of *Antigone;* even the great themes of classical and bourgeois literature can be represented and expressed by characters from the sphere of material production speaking an everyday language (Gerhart Hauptmann's *Weavers*). However, if this "translation" is to pierce and comprehend the everyday reality, it must be subjected to aesthetic stylization: it must be made into a novel, play, or story, in which every sentence has its own rhythm, its own weight. This stylization reveals the universal in the particular social situation, the ever recurring, desiring Subject in all objectivity. The revolution finds its limits and residue in this permanence which is preserved in art—preserved not as a piece of property, not as a bit of unchangeable nature, but as a remembrance of life past: remembrance of a life between illusion and reality, falsehood and truth, joy and death.

The specific social denominator, that which is "dated" in a work of art and surpassed by historical development, is the milieu, the *Lebenswelt* of the protagonists. It is precisely this *Lebenswelt* which is transcended by the protagonists—as Shakespeare's and Racine's princes transcend the courtly world of absolutism, as Stendhal's burghers transcend the bourgeois world, and Brecht's poor that of the proletariat. This transcendence occurs in the collision with their *Lebenswelt*, through events which appear in the context of particular social conditions while simultaneously revealing forces not attributable to these specific conditions. Dostoyevsky's *The Humiliated and the Offended*, Victor Hugo's *Les Misérables* suffer not only the injustice of a particular class society, they suffer the inhumanity of all times; they stand for humanity as such. The universal that appears in their fate is beyond that of class society. In fact, the latter is itself part of a world in which nature explodes the social framework. Eros and Thanatos assert their own power in and against the class struggle. Clearly, the class struggle is not always "responsible" for the fact that the "lovers do not remain together." [15] The convergence of fulfillment and death preserves its real power despite all romantic glorification and sociological explanation. The inexorable human entanglement in nature sustains its own dynamic in the given social relations and creates its own metasocial dimension.

Great literature knows a guiltless guilt which finds its first authentic expression in *Oedipus Rex*. Here is the domain of that which is changeable and that which is not. Obviously there are societies in which people no longer believe in oracles, and there may be societies in which there is no incest taboo, but it is difficult to imagine a society which has abolished what is called chance or fate, the encounter at the crossroads, the encounter of the lovers, but also the encounter with hell. Even in a technically all but perfect totalitarian system, only the forms of fate would change. Machines would operate not only as engines of control but also as engines of fate which would continue to show its force in the residue of still unconquered nature. Nature entirely controlled would deprive the machines of their stuff, their matter, on whose brute objectivity and resistance they depend.

The metasocial dimension is to a great extent rationalized in bourgeois literature; the catastrophe occurs in the confrontation between individual and society. Nevertheless, the social content remains secondary to the fate of the individuals. Does Balzac (the favorite example) in the *Comédie humaine* really portray the dynamic of finance and entrepreneurial capitalism in spite of his own "reactionary" political prejudices and preferences? To be sure, the society of his time comes to life in his work, but the aesthetic form has "absorbed" and transformed the social dynamic and made it the story of particular individuals—Lucien de Rubempré, Nucingen, Vautrin. They act and suffer in the society of their time, indeed they are representative of this society. However, the aesthetic quality of the *Comédie humaine* and its own truth is in the individualization of the social. In this transfiguration, the universal in the fate of the individuals shines through their specific social condition.

The life and death of individuals: even where the novel or the play articulates the struggle of the bourgeoisie against the aristocracy and the ascent of bourgeois liberties (Lessing's *Emilia Galotti,* Goethe's *Egmont,* the *Sturm und Drang,* Schiller's *Cabal and Love*), it is the personal fate which remains form-giving—the fate of the protagonists, not as participants in the class struggle, but as lovers, scoundrels, fools, and so on.

In Goethe's *Werther* the suicide is doubly determined. The lover experiences the tragedy of love (a tragedy which is not imposed merely by the predominant bourgeois morality), and the bourgeois suffers contempt at the hands of the nobility. Are the two motives interrelated in the structure of the work? The class content is sharply articulated: Lessing's *Emilia Galotti,* a drama of the militant bourgeoisie, lies open on the table in the room where Werther commits suicide. But the work as a whole is so much the story of the lovers and their own world that the bourgeois elements remain episodic.

This privatization of the social, the sublimation of reality, the idealization of love and death are often branded by Marxist aesthetics as conformist and repressive ideology. It condemns the transformation of social conflicts into personal fate, the abstraction from the class situation, the "elitist" character of the problems, the illusionary autonomy of the protagonists.

Such condemnation overlooks the critical potential which asserts itself precisely in the sublimation of the social content. Two worlds collide, each of which has its particular truth. Fiction creates its own reality which remains valid even when it is denied by the established reality. The right and wrong of individuals confront social right and wrong. Even in the most political works, this confrontation is not solely a political one; or rather the particular social confrontations are built into the play of metasocial forces between individual and individual, male and female, humanity and nature. The change in the mode of production would not cancel this dynamic. A free society could not "socialize" these forces, though it could emancipate individuals from their blind subjection to them.

History projects the image of a new world of liberation. Advanced capitalism has revealed real possibilities of liberation which surpass all traditional concepts. These possibilities have raised again the idea of the *end of art*. The radical possibilities of freedom (concretized in the emancipatory potential of technical progress) seem to make the traditional function of art obsolete, or at least to abolish it as a special branch of the division of labor, through the reduction of the separation between mental and manual labor. The images (*Schein*) of the Beautiful and of fulfillment would vanish when they are no longer denied by the society. In a free society the images become aspects of the real. Even now in the established society, the indictment and the promise preserved in art lose their unreal and utopian character to the degree to which they inform the strategy of oppositional movements (as they did in the sixties). While they do so in damaged and broken forms, they nevertheless indicate the qualitative difference from previous periods. This qualitative difference appears today in the protest against the definition of life as labor, in the struggle against the entire capitalist and state-socialist organization of work (the assembly line, Taylor system, hierarchy), in the struggle to end patriarchy, to reconstruct the destroyed life environment, and to develop and nurture a new morality and a new sensibility.

The realization of these goals is incompatible not only with a drastically reorganized capitalism, but also with a socialist society competing with capitalism on the latter's terms. The possibilities which reveal themselves today are rather those of a society organized under a new reality principle: existence would no longer be determined by the need for life-long alienated labor and leisure, human beings would no longer be subjected to the instruments of their labor, no longer dominated by the performances imposed upon them. The entire system of material and ideological repression and renunciation would be senseless.

But even such a society would not signal the end of art, the overcoming of tragedy, the reconciliation of the Dionysian and the Apollonian. Art cannot sever itself from its origins. It bears witness to the inherent limits of freedom and fulfillment, to human embeddedness in nature. In all its ideality art bears witness to the truth of dialectical materialism—the permanent non-identity between subject and object, individual and individual.

By virtue of its transhistorical, universal truths, art appeals to a consciousness which is not only that of a particular class, but that of human beings as "species beings," developing all their life-enhancing faculties. Who is the subject of this consciousness?

For Marxist aesthetics this subject is the proletariat which, as particular class, is the universal class. The emphasis is on the particular: the proletariat is the only class in capitalist society which has no interest in the preservation of the existing society. The proletariat is free from the values of this society and thus free for the liberation of all mankind. According to this conception, the consciousness of the proletariat would also be the consciousness that validates the truth of art. This theory corresponds to a situation which is no longer (or not yet) that prevailing in the advanced capitalist countries.

Lucien Goldmann has stated the central problem of Marxist aesthetics in the period of advanced capitalism. If the proletariat is not the negation of the existing society but to a great extent integrated into it, then Marxist aesthetics is confronted with a situation where "authentic forms of cultural creations" exist "though they cannot be attached to the consciousness—even a potential one—of a particular social group." The decisive question therefore is: how the "link is made between the economic structures and literary manifestations in a society where this link occurs *outside the collective consciousness*," i.e., without being grounded in a progressive class consciousness, without expressing such consciousness? [16]

Adorno answered: in such a situation the autonomy of art asserts itself in extreme form—as uncompromising estrangement. To both the integrated consciousness and also to reified Marxist aesthetics, the estranged works may well appear as elitist or as symptoms of decadence. But they are nevertheless authentic forms of contradictions, indicting the totality of a society which draws everything, even the estranging works, into its purview. This does not invalidate their truth nor deny their promise. To be sure, the "economic structures" assert themselves. They determine the use value (and with it the exchange value) of the works but not what they are and what they say.

Goldmann's text refers to a specific historical condition—the integration of the proletariat under advanced monopoly capitalism. But even if the proletariat were not integrated, its class consciousness would not be the privileged or the sole force which could preserve and reshape the truth of art. If art "is" for any collective consciousness at all, it is that of individuals united in their awareness of the universal need for liberation—regardless of their class position. Nietzsche's *Zarathustra* dedication "Für Alle und Keinen" (For All and None) may apply also to the truth of art.

Advanced capitalism constitutes class society

as a universe administered by a corrupt and heavily armed monopolistic class. To a large extent this totality also includes the socially coordinated needs and interests of the working class. If it is at all meaningful to speak of a mass base for art in capitalist society, this would refer only to pop art and best sellers. In the present, the subject to which authentic art appeals is socially anonymous; it does not coincide with the potential subject of revolutionary practice. And the more the exploited classes, "the people," succumb to the powers that be, the more will art be estranged from "the people." Art can preserve its truth, it can make conscious the necessity of change, only when it obeys its own law as against that of reality. Brecht, not exactly a partisan of the autonomy of art, writes: "A work which does not exhibit its sovereignty vis à vis reality and which does not bestow sovereignty upon the public vis à vis reality is not a work of art." [17]

But what appears in art as remote from the praxis of change demands recognition as a necessary element in a future praxis of liberation—as the "science of the beautiful," the "science of redemption and fulfillment." Art cannot change the world, but it can contribute to changing the consciousness and drives of the men and women who could change the world. The movement of the sixties tended toward a sweeping transformation of subjectivity and nature, of sensibility, imagination, and reason. It opened a new vista of things, an ingression of the superstructure into the base. Today the movement is encapsulated, isolated, and defensive, and an embarrassed leftist bureaucracy is quick to condemn the movement as impotent, intellectual elitism. Indeed, one prefers the safe regression to the collective father figure of a proletariat which is (understandably) not very interested in these problems. One insists on the commitment of art to a proletarian *Weltanschauung* oriented toward "the people." Revolutionary art is supposed to speak the "language of the people." Brecht wrote in the thirties: "There is only one ally against the growing barbarism, the people who suffer so much under it. Only from them can we expect something. Therefore it is incumbent [upon the writer] to turn to the people." And it is more necessary than ever to speak their language.[18] Sartre shares these sentiments: the intellectual must "regain as fast as possible the place that awaits him among the people." [19]

But who are "the people"? Brecht gives a very stringent definition: "the people who not only participate fully in the development but actually usurp it, force it, determine it. We envision a people which makes history, which changes the world and itself. We have a fighting people before our eyes . . ." [20] But in the advanced capitalist countries this "part of the people" is not "*the* people," not the large mass of the dependent population. Rather, "the people" as defined by Brecht would be a minority of the people, opposed to this mass, a militant minority. If art is supposed to be committed not only to this minority but to *the* people, then it is not clear why the writer must speak its language—it would not yet be the language of liberation.

It is characteristic that the texts just quoted commit art to "the people," that "the people" appear as the sole allies against barbarism. In both Marxist aesthetics and in the theory and propaganda of the New Left there is a strong tendency to speak of "the people" rather than of the proletariat. This tendency expresses the fact that under monopoly capitalism the exploited population is much larger than the "proletariat" and that it comprises a large part of previously independent strata of the middle class. If "the people" are dominated by the prevailing system of needs then only the rupture with this system can make "the people" an ally against barbarism. Prior to this rupture there is no "place among the people" which the writer can simply take up and which awaits him. Writers must rather first create this place, and this is a process which may require them to stand against the people, which may prevent them from speaking their language. In this sense "elitism" today may well have a radical content. To work for the radicalization of consciousness means to make explicit and conscious the material and ideological discrepancy between the writer and "the people" rather than to obscure and camouflage it. Revolutionary art may well become "The Enemy of the People."

The basic thesis that art must be a factor in changing the world can easily turn into its opposite if the tension between art and radical praxis is flattened out so that art loses its own dimension for change. A text of Brecht's clearly expresses this dialectic.[21] The title itself shows what happens when the antagonistic forces of art and praxis are harmonized. (The text is entitled: "The Art of Representing the World So That It Can Be Dominated.") But to show the transformed world as dominated means to show the continuity in change, means to obscure the qualitative difference between the new and the old. The goal is not the dominated but the liberated world. As if in recognition of this fact,

Brecht's text begins: "People who want to show the world as a possible object of domination are well advised at the outset not to speak of art, not to recognize the laws of art, not to aim at art." Why not? Perhaps because it is not the business of art to portray the world as the possible object of domination? Brecht's answer is: because art is "a power equipped with institutions and learned experts which will reluctantly accept only some of the new tendencies. Art can go no further without ceasing to be art." Nevertheless, says Brecht, "our philosophers" do not have to forgo entirely using the offices of art, "because it will undoubtedly be an art to represent the world so that it can be dominated." The essential tension between art and praxis is thus solved through the masterful play on the dual meaning of "art": as aesthetic form and as technique.

The necessity of the political struggle was from the beginning a presupposition of this essay. It is a truism that this struggle must be accompanied by a change of consciousness. But it must be recalled that this change is more than development of political consciousness—that it aims at a new "system of needs." Such a system would include a sensibility, imagination, and reason emancipated from the rule of exploitation. This emancipation, and the ways toward it, transcend the realm of propaganda. They are not adequately translatable into the language of political and economic strategy. Art is a productive force qualitatively different from labor; its essentially subjective qualities assert themselves against the hard objectivity of the class struggle. The writers who, *as artists,* identify themselves with the proletariat still remain outsiders—no matter how much they renounce the aesthetic form in favor of direct expression and communication. They remain outsiders not because of their nonproletarian background, their remoteness from the process of material production, their "elitism," and so on, but because of the essential transcendence of art which makes the conflict between art and political praxis inevitable. Surrealism in its revolutionary period testified to this inherent conflict between art and political realism. The possibility of an alliance between "the people" and art presupposes that the men and women administered by monopoly capitalism unlearn the language, concepts, and images of this administration, that they experience the dimension of qualitative change, that they reclaim their subjectivity, their inwardness.

Marxist literary criticism often displays scorn for "inwardness," for the dissection of the soul in bourgeois literature—a scorn which Brecht interpreted as a sign of revolutionary consciousness. But this attitude is not too remote from the scorn of the capitalists for an unprofitable dimension of life. If subjectivity is an "achievement" of the bourgeois era, it is at least an antagonistic force in capitalist society.

I have pointed out that the same applies to the critique of the individualism of bourgeois literature offered by Marxist aesthetics. To be sure, the concept of the bourgeois individual has become the ideological counterpoint to the competitive economic subject and the authoritarian head of the family. To be sure, the concept of the individual as developing freely in solidarity with others can become a reality only in a socialist society. But the fascist period and monopoly capitalism have decisively changed the political value of these concepts. The "flight into inwardness" and the insistence on a private sphere may well serve as bulwarks against a society which administers all dimensions of human existence. Inwardness and subjectivity may well become the inner and outer space for the subversion of experience, for the emergence of another universe. Today, the rejection of the individual as a "bourgeois" concept recalls and presages fascist undertakings. Solidarity and community do not mean absorption of the individual. They rather originate in autonomous individual decision; they unite freely associated individuals, not masses.

If the subversion of experience proper to art and the rebellion against the established reality principle contained in this subversion cannot be translated into political praxis, and if the radical potential of art lies precisely in this non-identity, then the question arises: how can this potential find valid representation in a work of art and how can it become a factor in the transformation of consciousness?

How can art speak the language of a radically different experience, how can it represent the qualitative difference? How can art invoke images and needs of liberation which reach into the depth dimension of human existence, how can it articulate the experience not only of a particular class, but of all the oppressed?

The qualitative difference of art does not constitute itself in the selection of a particular field where art could preserve its autonomy. Nor would it do to seek out a cultural area not yet occupied by the established society. Attempts have been made to argue that pornography and the obscene are islands of nonconformist communication. But such privileged areas do not exist. Both obscenity and pornography have long since been integrated. As commodities they too communicate the repressive whole.

Neither is the truth of art a matter of style alone. There is in art an abstract, illusory autonomy: private arbitrary invention of something new, a technique which remains extraneous to the content, or technique without content, form without matter. Such empty autonomy robs art of its own concreteness which pays tribute to that which is, even in its negation. In its very elements (word, color, tone) art depends on the transmitted cultural material; art shares it with the existing society. And no matter how much art overturns the ordinary meanings of words and images, the transfiguration is still that of a given material. This is the case even when the words are broken, when new ones are invented—otherwise all communication would be severed. This limitation of aesthetic autonomy is the condition under which art can become a social factor.

In this sense art is inevitably part of that which is and only as part of that which is does it speak against that which is. This contradiction is preserved and resolved (*aufgehoben*) in the aesthetic form which gives the familiar content and the familiar experience the power of estrangement—and which leads to the emergence of a new consciousness and a new perception.

Aesthetic form is not opposed to content, not even dialectically. In the work of art, form becomes content and vice versa.

The price of being an artist is to experience that which all non-artists call form, as content, as "the real thing" (*die Sache selbst*). Then however one belongs to an inverted world; because now the content, our own life included, becomes something merely formal.[22]

A play, a novel become literary works by virtue of the form which "incorporates" and sublimates "the stuff." The latter may be the "starting point of aesthetic transformation." [23] It may contain the "motive" of this transformation, it may be class determined—but in the work this "stuff," divested of its immediacy, becomes something qualitatively different, part of another reality. Even where a fragment of reality is left untransformed (for example, quoted phrases from a speech by Robespierre) the content is changed by the work as a whole; its meaning can even be turned into its opposite.

The "tyranny of form"—in an authentic work a necessity prevails which demands that no line, no sound could be replaced (in the optimal case, which doesn't exist). This inner necessity (the quality which distinguishes authentic from inauthentic works) is indeed tyranny inasmuch as it suppresses the immediacy of expression. But what is here suppressed is false immediacy: false to the degree to which it drags along the unreflected mystified reality.

In defense of aesthetic form, Brecht notes in 1921:

> I observe that I am beginning to become a classic. Those extreme forced efforts [of expressionism] to spew forth with all means certain (banal or soon to be banal) content! One blames the classics for their service to form and overlooks that it is the form which is the servant here.[24]

Brecht connects the destruction of form with banalization. To be sure, this connection does not do justice to expressionism, much of which was by no means banal. But Brecht's verdict recalls the essential relation between aesthetic form and the estrangement effect: the deliberately formless expression "banalizes" inasmuch as it obliterates the opposition to the established universe of discourse—an opposition which is crystallized in the aesthetic form.

The submission to aesthetic form is the vehicle of the nonconformist sublimation, which accompanies the desublimation described earlier. (See p. 7, above.) Their unity constitutes itself in the work. The ego and the id, instinctual goals and emotions, rationality and imagination are withdrawn from their socialization by a repressive society and strive toward autonomy—albeit in a fictitious world. But the encounter with the fictitious world restructures consciousness and gives sensual representation to a counter-societal experience. The aesthetic sublimation thus liberates and validates childhood and adult dreams of happiness and sorrow.

Not only poetry and drama but also the realistic novel must transform the reality which is their material in order to re-present its essence as envisioned by art. Any historical reality can become "the stage" for such mimesis. The only requirement is that it must be *stylized*, subjected to aesthetic "formation." And precisely this stylization allows the transvaluation of the norms of the established reality principle—de-sublimation on the basis of the original sublimation, dissolution of the social taboos, of the social management of Eros and Thanatos. Men and women speak and act with less inhibition than under the weight of daily life; they are more shameless (but also more embarrassed) in their loving and hating; they are loyal to their passions even when destroyed by them. But they are also more conscious, more reflective, more lovable, and more contemptible. And the objects in their world are more transparent, more independent, and more compelling.

Mimesis is representation through estrangement, subversion of consciousness. Experience is intensified to the breaking point; the world appears as it does for Lear and Antony, Berenice, Michael Kohlhaas, Woyzeck, as it does for the lovers of all times. They experience the world demystified. The intensification of perception can go as far as to distort things so that the unspeakable is spoken, the otherwise invisible becomes visible, and the unbearable explodes. Thus the aesthetic transformation turns into indictment—but also into a celebration of that which resists injustice and terror, and of that which can still be saved.

The mimesis in literature occurs in the medium of language; it is tightened or loosened, forced to yield insights otherwise obscured. Prose is subjected to its own rhythm. What is normally not spoken is said; what is normally spoken too much remains unsaid if it conceals that which is essential. Restructuring takes place through concentration, exaggeration, emphasis on the essential, reordering of facts. The bearer of these qualities is not the particular sentence, not its words, not its syntax; the bearer is the whole. It is only the whole which bestows upon these elements their aesthetic meaning and function.

Critical mimesis finds expression in the most manifold forms. It is found both in the language of Brecht, which is formed by the immediacy of the need for change, and in the schizophrenically diagnostic language of Beckett, in which there is no talk of change. The indictment is just as much in the sensuous, emotional language of *Werther* and the *Fleurs du Mal* as it is in the hardness of Stendhal and Kafka.

The indictment does not exhaust itself in the recognition of evil; art is also the promise of liberation. This promise, too, is a quality of aesthetic form, or more precisely, of the beautiful as a quality of aesthetic form. The promise is wrested from established reality. It invokes an image of the end of power, the appearance (*Schein*) of freedom. But only the appearance; clearly, the fulfillment of this promise is not within the domain of art.

Are there, can there be, authentic works in which the Antigones finally destroy the Creons, in which the peasants defeat the princes, in which love is stronger than death? This reversal of history is a regulative idea in art, in the loyalty sustained (until death) to the vision of a better world, a vision which remains true even in defeat. At the same time, art militates against the notion of an iron progress, against blind confidence in a humanity which will eventually assert itself. Otherwise the work of art and its claim to truth would be lies.

In the transforming mimesis, the image of liberation is fractured by reality. If art were to promise that at the end good would triumph over evil, such a promise would be refuted by the historical truth. In reality it is evil which triumphs, and there are only islands of good where one can find refuge for a brief time. Authentic works of art are aware of this; they reject the promise made too easily; they refuse the unburdened happy end. They must reject it, for the realm of freedom lies beyond mimesis. The happy ending is "the other" of art. Where it nevertheless appears, as in Shakespeare, as in Goethe's *Iphigenie*, as in the finale of *Figaro* or *Falstaff,* as in Proust, it seems to be denied by the work as a whole. In *Faust* the happy end is only and merely in heaven, and the great comedy cannot free itself from the tragedy which it attempts to banish. Mimesis remains re-presentation of reality. This bondage resists the utopian quality of art: sorrow and unfreedom are still reflected in the purest imagery of happiness and freedom. They too contain the protest against the reality in which they are destroyed.

Actually it is not a question of the happy *end;* what is decisive is the work as a whole. It preserves the remembrance of things past. They may be superseded (*aufgehoben*) in the resolution of the tragic conflict, in the fulfillment attained. But though superseded they remain present in the anxiety for the future. An example from Ibsen: the most "bourgeois" of the great dramatists has *The Lady from the Sea* return to her marriage by her own free decision; she turns away from the Stranger with whom she has shared the adventure of the sea; she now seeks fulfillment in the family. But the play as a whole contradicts this solution. Ellida's freedom has its limit in the impossibility of undoing the past. This impossibility is not the fault of class society; it is grounded in the irreversibility of time, in the unconquerable objectivity and lawfulness of nature.

Art cannot redeem its promise, and reality offers no promises, only chances. We are back at the traditional concept of art as illusion (*Schein*) though perhaps beautiful illusion (*schöner Schein*). True, but bourgeois aesthetics has always understood appearance (*Schein*) as the appearance of truth, a truth proper to art, and has divested the given reality of its claim to total legitimation. Thus there are two realities and two modes of truth. Cognition and experience are antagonistically divided, for art as illusion (*Schein*) has cognitive content and function. Art's unique truth breaks with both everyday and holiday reality, which block a whole dimension of society and nature. Art is transcendence into this dimension where its autonomy constitutes itself as autonomy in contradiction. When art abandons this autonomy and with it the aesthetic form in which the autonomy is expressed, art succumbs to that reality which it seeks to grasp and indict. While the abandonment of the aesthetic form may well provide the most immediate, most direct mirror of a society in which subjects and objects are shattered, atomized, robbed of their words and images, the rejection of the aesthetic sublimation turns such works into bits and pieces of the very society whose "anti-art" they want to be. Anti-art is self-defeating from the outset.

The various phases and trends of anti-art or non-art share a common assumption—namely, that the modern period is characterized by a disintegration of reality which renders any self-enclosed form, any intention of meaning (*Sinngebung*) un-

true, if not impossible.[25] The collage, or the juxtaposition of media, or the renunciation of any aesthetic mimesis are held to be adequate responses
to given reality, which, disjoined and fragmented,
militates against any aesthetic formation. This
assumption is in flat contradiction to the actual
state of affairs. Rather, the opposite is the case.
We are experiencing, not the destruction of every
whole, every unit or unity, every meaning, but rather
the rule and power of the whole, the superimposed,
administered unification. Not disintegration but
reproduction and integration of that which is, is
the catastrophe. And in the intellectual culture of
our society, it is the aesthetic form which, by virtue
of its otherness, can stand up against this integration. Significantly, Peter Weiss's recent book has
the title *Aesthetik des Widerstands* (The Aesthetics
of Resistance).

The artist's desperate effort to make art a direct
expression of life cannot overcome the separation
of art from life. Wellershoff states the decisive fact:
"unbridgeable social differences exist between the
can factory and the studio of the artist: Warhol's
factory";[26] between action painting and the real life
which is going on around it. Nor can these differences be bridged by simply letting things happen

(noises, movements, chitchat, etc.) and incorporating them, unaltered, into a definite "frame" (e.g., a concert hall, a book). The immediacy thus expressed is false inasmuch as it results from a mere abstraction from the real-life context which establishes this immediacy. The latter is thus mystified: it does not appear as what it is and does—it is a synthetic, artistic immediacy.

The release (*Entschränkung*) and desublimation which occur in anti-art thus abstract from (and falsify) reality because they lack the cognitive and cutting power of the aesthetic form; they are mimesis without transformation. Collage, montage, dislocation do not change this fact. The exhibition of a soup can communicates nothing about the life of the worker who produced it, nor of that of the consumer. Renunciation of the aesthetic form does not cancel the difference between art and life—but it does cancel that between essence and appearance, in which the truth of art has its home and which determines the political value of art. The desublimation of art is supposed to release spontaneity—of both the artist and the recipient. But just as, in radical praxis, spontaneity can advance the movement of liberation only as mediated spontaneity, that is, resulting from the transformation of consciousness—so also in art. Without this dual transformation (of the subjects and their world), the desublimation of art can lead only to making the artist superfluous without *democratizing* and *generalizing creativity*.

In this sense, renunciation of the aesthetic form is abdication of responsibility. It deprives art of the very form in which it can create that other reality within the established one—the cosmos of hope.

The political program of the abolition of artistic autonomy leads to a "leveling of the stages of reality between art and life." It is only this surrender of its autonomous status which enables art to infiltrate "the ensemble of use values." This process is ambivalent. "It can just as easily signify the degeneration of art into commercialized mass culture as, on the other hand, transform itself into a subversive counterculture." [27] But this latter alternative seems questionable. A subversive counterculture today is conceivable only in contradiction to the prevailing art industry and its heteronomous art. That is to say, a real counterculture would have to insist on the autonomy of art, on its *own* autonomous art. Consequently, would not an art which rebels against integration into the market necessarily appear as "elitist"? "In the face of the decreasing use value of a totally marketed literature, the anachronistic-elitist notion of *Dichten* as a distinguished 'higher' art assumes again an all but *subversive* character." [28]

The work of art can attain political relevance only as autonomous work. The aesthetic form is essential to its social function. The qualities of the form negate those of the repressive society—the qualities of its life, labor, and love.

Aesthetic quality and political tendency are inherently interrelated, but their unity is not immediate. Walter Benjamin formulated the inner relation between tendency and quality in the thesis: "The tendency of a literary work can be politically correct only if it is also correct by literary standards." [29] This formulation rejects clearly enough vulgar Marxist aesthetics. But it does not solve the difficulty implied in Benjamin's concept of literary "correctness"—namely, his identification of literary and political quality in the domain of art. This identification harmonizes the tension between literary form and political content: the perfect literary form transcends correct political tendency; the unity of tendency and quality is antagonistic.

IV

The world intended in art is never and nowhere merely the given world of everyday reality, but neither is it a world of mere fantasy, illusion, and so on. It contains nothing that does not also exist in the given reality, the actions, thoughts, feelings, and dreams of men and women, their potentialities and those of nature. Nevertheless the world of a work of art is "unreal" in the ordinary sense of this word: it is a fictitious reality. But it is "unreal" not because it is less, but because it is more as well as qualitatively "other" than the established reality. As fictitious world, as illusion (*Schein*), it contains more truth than does everyday reality. For the latter is mystified in its institutions and relationships, which make necessity into choice, and alienation into self-realization. Only in the "illusory world" do things appear as what they are and what they can be. By virtue of this truth (which art alone can express in sensuous representation) the world is inverted— it is the given reality, the ordinary world which now appears as untrue, as false, as deceptive reality.

The world of art as the *appearance* of truth, the everyday reality as untrue, delusion; this thesis of idealistic aesthetics has found scandalizing formulations:

> ... the entire sphere of the empirical inner and
> outer reality is to be called, in a stronger sense
> than that reserved for art, the world of mere
> illusion and a bitterer deception, rather than the
> world of reality. True reality is to be found
> only beyond the immediacy of sensation and of
> external objects.[30]

Dialectical logic may provide meaning and justification for these claims. They have their materialistic
truth in Marx's analysis of the divergence of essence
and appearance in capitalist society. But in the
confrontation between art and reality they become
mockery. Auschwitz and My Lai, the torture,
starvation, and dying—is this entire world supposed
to be "mere illusion" and "bitterer deception"? It
remains rather the "bitterer" and all but unim-
aginable reality. Art draws away from this reality,
because it cannot represent this suffering without
subjecting it to aesthetic form, and thereby to the
mitigating catharsis, to enjoyment. Art is inexorably
infested with this guilt. Yet this does not release
art from the necessity of recalling again and again
that which can survive even Auschwitz and perhaps
one day make it impossible. If even this memory

were to be silenced, then the "end of art" would indeed have come. Authentic art preserves this memory in spite of and against Auschwitz; this memory is the ground in which art has always originated—this memory and the need to create images of the possible "other." Deception and illusion have been qualities of established reality throughout recorded history. And mystification is a feature not only of *capitalist* society. The work of art on the other hand does not conceal that which is—it reveals.

The possible "other" which appears in art is transhistorical inasmuch as it transcends any and every specific historical situation. Tragedy is always and everywhere while the satyr play follows it always and everywhere; joy vanishes faster than sorrow. This insight, inexorably expressed in art, may well shatter faith in progress but it may also keep alive another image and another goal of praxis, namely the reconstruction of society and nature under the principle of increasing the human potential for happiness. The revolution is for the sake of life, not death. Here is the perhaps most profound kinship between art and revolution. Lenin's resolution to be incapable of listening to the Beethoven sonatas which he admired so much testifies to the truth of art. Lenin himself knew it— and rejected this knowledge.

> . . . all too often I cannot listen to music. It works on one's nerves. One would rather babble nonsense, and caress the heads of people who live in a dirty hell and who nevertheless can create such beauty. But today one should not caress anyone's heads—one's hand would be bitten off. One must beat heads, beat unmercifully—although ideally we are against all violence.[31]

Indeed art does not stand under the law of revolutionary strategy. But perhaps the latter will one day incorporate some of the truth inherent in art. Lenin's phrase "one would rather" expresses not a personal preference but an historical alternative—a utopia to be translated into reality.

There is in art inevitably an element of *hubris:* art cannot translate its vision into reality. It remains a "fictitious" world, though as such it sees through and anticipates reality. Thus art corrects its ideality: the hope which it represents ought not to remain mere ideal. This is the hidden categorical imperative of art. Its realization lies outside of art. To be sure, the "pure humanity" of Goethe's *Iphigenie* is realized in the farewell scene of the play—but only there, in the play itself. It is absurd to conclude that we need more Iphigenies who preach the gospel of pure humanity, and more kings who accept it. Moreover, we have known for a long time that pure humanity does not redeem all human afflictions and crimes; rather it becomes their victim. Thus it remains ideal: the degree of its realization depends on the political struggle. The ideal enters this struggle only as end, *telos;* it transcends the given praxis. But the images of the ideal itself change with the changing political struggle. Today, "pure humanity" has perhaps found its truest literary representation in the deaf-mute daughter of *Mother Courage,* who is killed by a gang of soldiers while she is saving the town through her drumming.

The question now arises: are the transcending, critical elements of the aesthetic form also operative in those works of art which are predominantly affirmative? And vice versa: does extreme negation in art still contain affirmation?

The aesthetic form, by virtue of which a work stands against established reality, is, at the same time, a form of affirmation through the reconciling catharsis. This catharsis is an ontological rather than psychological event. It is grounded in the specific qualities of the form itself, its non-repressive order, its cognitive power, its image of suffering that has come to an end. But the "solution," the reconciliation which the catharsis offers, also preserves the irreconcilable. The internal relation between the two poles can be illustrated by two examples of extreme affirmation and extreme negation—the "Türmerlied" (Song of the Tower Warden) in *Goethe's Faust:*

Ihr glücklichen Augen,	Dear eyes, you so happy,
Was je ihr geseh'n,	Whatever you've seen,
Es sei wie es wolle,	No matter its nature,
Es war doch so schön.	So fair has it been.[32]

and the last words in the last scene of Wedekind's *Pandora's Box:*

Es war doch so schön!

Can one still speak of aesthetic affirmation in this last scene? In the dirty attic-room where Jack the Ripper does his thing, the horror comes to an end. Does the catharsis even here still have the power of affirmation? The last words of the dying Duchess Geschwitz ("O verflucht!") are a curse pronounced in the name of love—love brutally destroyed and humiliated. The final outcry is that of rebellion; it affirms in all that horror the powerless power of love. Even here, in the hands of the killer and beside the slaughtered body of the beloved Lulu, a woman utters the cry for the eternity of joy: "Mein Engel!—Lass dich noch einmal sehen! Ich bin dir nah! Bleibe dir nah—in Ewigkeit! . . . O verflucht!" (Angel!—Let me look at you once again! I am close. I will stay close to you—in eternity . . . Damn it!) Similarly in Strindberg's most terrifying plays, where men and women seem to live only from hatred, emptiness, and malice, the cry from the *Dreamplay* resounds: "Es ist schade um die Menschen." (It is a pity about human beings.)

Does this unity of affirmation and negation also prevail in the exuberantly Apollonian "Song of the Tower Warden"? The "whatever you've seen" invokes the memory of pain past. Happiness has the last word, but it is a word of remembrance. And, in the last line, the affirmation carries a tone of sorrow—and of defiance.

In his analysis of Goethe's poem *Über allen Gipfeln . . . ,*[33] Adorno has shown how the highest literary form preserves the memory of anguish in the moment of peace:

> The greatest lyric works owe their dignity pre-
> cisely to the force with which in them the Ego,
> stepping back from alienation, invokes the
> appearance [*Schein*] of nature. Their pure sub-
> jectivity, that which seems unbroken and
> harmonious in them, testifies to the opposite:
> to the suffering in an existence alien to the
> subject, as well as to the love of this existence.
> Indeed their harmony is actually nothing but
> the accord between such suffering and such love.
> Even the "Warte nur, balde/ruhest du auch"
> has the gesture of consolation: its abysmal beauty
> cannot be separated from that which it keeps
> silent: the image of a world which refuses peace.
> Only because the tone of the poem sympathizes
> with this sorrow, can it insist that there ought
> to be peace.[34]

Aesthetic formation proceeds under the law of the Beautiful, and the dialectic of affirmation and negation, consolation and sorrow is the dialectic of the Beautiful.

Marxist aesthetics has sharply rejected the idea of the Beautiful, the central category of "bourgeois" aesthetics. It seems difficult indeed to associate this concept with revolutionary art; it seems irresponsible, snobbish to speak of the Beautiful in the face of the necessities of the political struggle. Moreover, the Establishment has created and effectively sold beauty in the form of plastic purity and loveliness—an extension of exchange values to the aesthetic-erotic dimension. Nevertheless, in contrast to such conformist realizations, the idea of Beauty appears time and again in progressive movements, as an aspect of the reconstruction of nature and society. What are the sources of this radical potential?

They are first in the erotic quality of the Beautiful, which persists through all changes in the "judgment of taste." As pertaining to the domain of Eros, the Beautiful represents the pleasure principle. Thus, it rebels against the prevailing reality principle of domination. The work of art speaks the liberating language, invokes the liberating images of the subordination of death and destruction to the will to live. This is the emancipatory element in aesthetic affirmation.

However, in a certain sense, the Beautiful seems to be "neutral." It can be a quality of a regressive as well as progressive (social) totality. One can speak of the beauty of a fascist feast. (Leni Riefenstahl has filmed it!) But the neutrality of the Beautiful shows itself as deception if what it suppresses or conceals is recognized. The directness and immediacy of the visual presentation impedes this recognition; it can repress the imagination.

In contrast, the representation of fascism becomes possible in literature because the word, not silenced or overwhelmed by the picture, carries freely the recognition and the indictment. But the cognitive mimesis can reach only the protagonists and their henchmen—not the system they incorporate, nor the horror of the whole, which are beyond the banishing power of the cathartic mimesis. Thus, the stylization petrifies the lords of the terror into monuments that survive—blocks of memory not to be surrendered to oblivion.

In a number of works (for example Brecht's poems, his *The Resistible Ascent of Arturo Ui*, and *Fear and Misery of the Third Reich;* Sartre's

The Condemned of Altona; Günter Grass's *Dog Years;* Paul Celan's *Death Fugue*), the transforming mimesis terminates in the recognition of the infamous reality of fascism, in its daily concreteness, underneath its world historical appearance. And this recognition is a triumph: in the aesthetic form (of the play, the poem, the novel), the terror is called up, called by its name, and made to testify, to denounce itself. It is only a moment of triumph, a moment in the stream of consciousness. But the form has captured it and has given it permanence. By virtue of this achievement of mimesis, these works contain the quality of Beauty in its perhaps most sublimated form: as political Eros. In the creation of an aesthetic form, in which the horror of fascism continues to cry out in spite of all forces of repression and forgetting, the life instincts rebel against the global sado-masochistic phase of contemporary civilization. The return of the repressed, achieved and preserved in the work of art, may intensify this rebellion.

The accomplished work of art perpetuates the memory of the moment of gratification. And the work of art is beautiful to the degree to which it opposes its own order to that of reality—its non-repressive order where even the curse is still spoken in the name of Eros. It appears in the brief moments of fulfillment, tranquility—in the "beautiful moment" which arrests the incessant dynamic and disorder, the constant need to do all that which has to be done in order to continue living.

The Beautiful belongs to the imagery of liberation:

> When I walked up the valley yesterday, I saw two girls sitting on a rock: one was binding up her hair, the other helped her; and the golden hair hung down, and a serious pale face, and yet so young, and the black dress, and the other so eager to help. . . . One might wish at times to be a Medusa's head to change such a group into stone so people can see it. They got up, the beautiful group was destroyed; but as they so descended between the rocks, it was yet another picture. The most beautiful pictures, the most swelling tones regroup, dissolve. Only one thing remains: an infinite beauty, which passes from one form to another.[35]

In this constant "regrouping and dissolving" of the beautiful moments, each of them is irretrievably lost when it passes. In passing, it invokes the

coming of still another moment of fulfillment, of
peace. Thus, the defiant remembrance is alleviated,
and the Beautiful becomes part of the affirmative,
reconciling catharsis. Art is powerless against this
reconciliation with the irreconcilable; it is inherent in the aesthetic form itself. Under its law,
"even the cry of despair . . . still pays its tribute
to the infamous affirmation" and a representation
of the most extreme suffering "still contains the
potential to wring out enjoyment." [36] Thus even
the prison scene in *Faust* is beautiful, as is the lucid
madness in Büchner's *Lenz,* Therese's story of the
death of her mother in Kafka's *Amerika,* and
Beckett's *Endgame.*

The sensuous substance of the Beautiful is
preserved in aesthetic sublimation. The autonomy
of art and its political potential manifest themselves
in the cognitive and emancipatory power of this
sensuousness. It is therefore not surprising that,
historically, the attack on autonomous art is linked
with the denunciation of sensuousness in the name
of morality and religion.

Horst Bredekamp has shown that the sys-
tematic mobilization of the populace against the
emancipation of art from religious ritual has its
roots in the ascetic movements of the High Middle

Ages. Autonomous art is condemned as infamous sensuality. "Release of aesthetic-sensuous stimuli," "artistic tickling of the senses" are presented as "basic conditions for the autonomization of art." The burning of paintings and statues is not an "expression of a blindly raging fanaticism," but rather a "consequence of a petty bourgeois, anti-intellectualistic ideal of life; Savonarola is its uncompromising representative." [37] Similarly Adorno: "hostility against happiness, asceticism, that sort of ethos which constantly babbles names like Luther and Bismarck, does not want aesthetic autonomy." [38] Adorno finds here traces of the "petty bourgeois' hatred of sex."

The medium of sensibility also constitutes the paradoxical relation of art to time—paradoxical because what is experienced through the medium of sensibility is present, while art cannot show the present without showing it as past. What has become form in the work of art has happened: it is recalled, re-presented. The mimesis translates reality into memory. In this remembrance, art has recognized what is and what could be, within and beyond the social conditions. Art has rescued this knowledge from the sphere of abstract concept and embedded it in the realm of sensuousness.

Its cognitive power draws its strength from this realm. The sensuous force of the Beautiful keeps the promise alive—memory of the happiness that once was, and that seeks its return.

Though the universe of art is permeated with death, art spurns the temptation to give death a meaning. For art, death is a constant hazard, misfortune, a constant threat even in moments of happiness, triumph, fulfillment. (Even in *Tristan,* death remains an accident, a double accident of the love potion and of the wound. The hymn on death is a hymn on love.) All suffering becomes sickness unto death—though the disease itself may be cured. *La Mort des Pauvres* may well be liberation; poverty can be abolished. Still, death remains the negation inherent in society, in history. It is the final re-membrance of things past—last remembrance of all possibilities forsaken, of all that which could have been said and was not, of every gesture, every tenderness not shown. But death also recalls the false tolerance, the ready compliance with the necessity of pain.

Art declares its *caveat* to the thesis according to which the time has come to change the world. While art bears witness to the necessity of liberation, it also testifies to its limits. What has been done cannot be undone; what has passed cannot be recaptured. History is guilt but not redemption. Eros and Thanatos are lovers as well as adversaries. Destructive energy may be brought into the service of life to an ever higher degree—Eros itself lives under the sign of finitude, of pain. The "eternity of joy" constitutes itself through the death of individuals. For them, this eternity is an abstract universal. And, perhaps, the eternity does not last very long. The world was not made for the sake of the human being and it has not become more human.

Inasmuch as art preserves, with the promise of happiness, the memory of the goals that failed, it can enter, as a "regulative idea," the desperate struggle for changing the world. Against all fetishism of the productive forces, against the continued enslavement of individuals by the objective conditions (which remain those of domination), art represents the ultimate goal of all revolutions: the freedom and happiness of the individual.

Conclusion

Marxist theory comprehends the established society as a reality to be changed. In any case, socialism could at least be a better society in which human beings could enjoy both more liberty and more happiness. To the degree to which administered human beings today reproduce their own repression and eschew a rupture with the given reality, to this degree revolutionary theory acquires an abstract character. The goal, socialism as a better society, also appears as abstract—ideological in relation to the radical praxis which necessarily operates within the concreteness of the established society.

In this situation the affinity, and the opposition, between art and radical praxis become surprisingly clear. Both envision a universe which, while originating in the given social relationships, also liberates individuals from these relationships. This vision appears as the permanent future of revolutionary praxis. The notion of the continuation of the class struggle under socialism expresses this point, albeit in a distorted form. The permanent transformation of society under the principle of freedom is necessitated not only by the continued existence of class interests. The institutions of a socialist society, even in their most democratic form, could never resolve all the conflicts between the universal and the particular, between human beings and nature, between individual and individual. Socialism does not and cannot liberate Eros from Thanatos. Here is the limit which drives the revolution beyond any accomplished stage of freedom: it is the struggle for the impossible, against the unconquerable whose domain can perhaps nevertheless be reduced.

Art reflects this dynamic in its insistence on its own truth, which has its ground in social reality and is yet its "other." Art breaks open a dimension inaccessible to other experience, a dimension in which human beings, nature, and things no longer stand under the law of the established reality principle. Subjects and objects encounter the appearance of that autonomy which is denied them in their society. The encounter with the truth of art happens in the estranging language and images which make perceptible, visible, and audible that which is no longer, or not yet, perceived, said, and heard in everyday life.

The autonomy of art reflects the unfreedom of individuals in the unfree society. If people were free, then art would be the form and expression of their freedom. Art remains marked by unfreedom; in contradicting it, art achieves its autonomy. The *nomos* which art obeys is not that of the established reality principle but of its negation. But mere negation would be abstract, the "bad" utopia. The utopia in great art is never the simple negation of the reality principle but its transcending preservation (*Aufhebung*) in which past and present cast their shadow on fulfillment. The authentic utopia is grounded in recollection.

"All reification is a forgetting."[39] Art fights reification by making the petrified world speak, sing, perhaps dance. Forgetting past suffering and past joy alleviates life under a repressive reality principle. In contrast, remembrance spurs the drive for the conquest of suffering and the permanence of joy. But the force of remembrance is frustrated: joy itself is overshadowed by pain. Inexorably so? The horizon of history is still open. If the remembrance of things past would become a motive power in the struggle for changing the world, the struggle would be waged for a revolution hitherto suppressed in the previous historical revolutions.

Notes

1. Especially among the authors of the periodicals *Kursbuch* (Frankfurt: Suhrkamp, later Rotbuch Verlag), *Argument* (Berlin), *Literaturmagazin* (Reinbek: Rowohlt). In the center of this discussion is the idea of an autonomous art in confrontation with the capitalist art industry on the one hand, and the radical propaganda art on the other. See especially the excellent articles by Nicolas Born, H. C. Buch, Wolfgang Harich, Hermann Peter Piwitt, and Michael Schneider in volumes I and II of the *Literaturmagazin*, the volume *Autonomie der Kunst* (Frankfurt: Suhrkamp, 1972) and Peter Bürger, *Theorie der Avantgarde* (Frankfurt: Suhrkamp, 1974).

2. See Erich Köhler, *Ideal und Wirklichkeit in der Höfischen Epik* (Tübingen: Niemeyer, 1956; second edition 1970), especially chapter V, for a discussion of this in relation to the courtly epic.

3. See pp. 55f.

4. See my *Counterrevolution and Revolt* (Boston: Beacon Press, 1972), p. 81.

5. Ernst Fischer in *Auf den Spuren der Wirklichkeit; sechs Essays* (Reinbek: Rowohlt, 1968) recognizes in the "will to form" (*Wille zur Gestalt*) the will to transcend the actual: negation of that which is, and presentiment (*Ahnung*) of a freer and purer existence. In this sense, art is the "irreconcilable, the resistance of the human being to its vanishing in the [established] order and systems" (p. 67).

6. "Two antagonistic attitudes toward the powers that be are prevalent in literature: *resistance* and *submission*. Literature is certainly not mere ideology

and does not merely express a social consciousness that invokes the illusion of harmony, assuring the individuals that everything is as it ought to be, and that nobody has the right to expect fate to give him more than he receives. To be sure, literature has time and again justified established social relationships; nevertheless, it has always kept alive that human yearning which cannot find gratification in the existing society. Grief and sorrow are essential elements of bourgeois literature" (Leo Lowenthal, *Das Bild des Menschen in der Literatur* [Neuwied: Luchterhand, 1966] pp. 14f.). (Published in English as *Literature and the Image of Man* [Boston: Beacon Press 1957].)

7. See my essay "The Affirmative Character of Culture" in *Negations* (Boston: Beacon Press, 1968).

8. In his book *Marxistische Ideologie und allgemeine Kunsttheorie* (Tübingen: Mohr, 1970), Hans-Dietrich Sander presents a thorough analysis of Marx's and Engels' contribution to a theory of art. The provocative conclusion: most of Marxist aesthetics is not only a gross vulgarization—Marx's and Engels' views are also turned into their opposite! He writes: Marx and Engels saw "the essence of a work of art precisely not in its political or social relevance" (p. 174). They are closer to Kant, Fichte, and Schelling than to Hegel (p. 171). Sander's documentation for this thesis may well be too selective and minimize statements by Marx and Engels which contradict Sander's interpretation. However, his analysis does show clearly the difficulty of Marxist aesthetics in coming to grips with the problems of the theory of art.

9. Bertolt Brecht, "Volkstümlichkeit und Realismus," in *Gesammelte Werke* (Frankfurt: Suhrkamp, 1967), volume VIII, p. 323.

10. Georg Lukács, "Es geht um den Realismus," in *Marxismus und Literatur,* edited by Fritz J. Raddatz (Reinbek: Rowohlt, 1969), volume II, p. 77.

11. In *Die Linkskurve* III, 5 (Berlin: May 1931, reprinted 1970), p. 17.

12. *Colloque international sur la sociologie de la littérature* (Bruxelles: Institut de la Sociologie, 1974), p. 40.

13. Walter Benjamin, "Fragment über Methodenfrage einer Marxistischen Literatur-Analyse," in *Kursbuch* 20 (Frankfurt: Suhrkamp, 1970), p. 3.

14. Leo Lowenthal, *Das Bild des Menschen in der Literatur,* p. 12.

15. Reinhard Lettau on Bob Dylan's "Nashville Skyline," in *Der Spiegel,* 1974/3, p. 112.

16. Lucien Goldmann, *Towards a Sociology of the Novel* (London: Tavistock Publ., 1975), pp. 10f.

17. Brecht, *Gesammelte Werke* op. cit., volume VIII, p. 411.

18. Ibid., p. 323.

19. Jean-Paul Sartre, *On a raison de se révolter* (Paris: Gallimard, 1974), p. 96.

20. Brecht, *Gesammelte Werke,* op. cit., pp. 324f.

21. Brecht, *Gesammelte Werke,* volume VII, pp. 260f.

22. Friedrich Nietzsche, *Der Wille zur Macht* (Stuttgart: Kröner, 1930), p. 552.

23. K. A. Wittfogel, in *Die Linkskurve* II, ii

(Berlin, November 1930, reprinted 1970), p. 9.
24. *Tagebücher* 1920–1922 (Frankfurt Suhrkamp, 1975), p. 138.
25. See Dieter Wellershoff's critical analysis in *Die Auflösung des Kunstbegriffs* (Frankfurt: Suhrkamp, 1976).
26. Wellershoff, *Die Auflösung des Kunstbegriffs,* p. 39.
27. Jürgen Habermas, *Legitimation Crisis* (Boston: Beacon Press, 1975), pp. 85f.
28. Michael Schneider, in *Literaturmagazin* II, (Reinbek: Rowohlt, 1974), p. 265.
29. Walter Benjamin, "Der Autor als Produzent," in Raddatz, *Marxismus und Literatur,* volume II, p. 264.
30. Hegel, "Vorlesungen über die Aesthetic" in *Sämtliche Werke* XII (Stuttgart: Fromnan, 1927), p. 28. Published in English as *The Philosophy of Fine Art I* (London: Bell, 1920), p. 10.
31. Gorki's "Erinnerungen an Zeitgenossen," in Sander, *Marxistische Ideologie und allgemeine Kunsttheorie,* p. 86.
32. Goethe, *Faust,* part II, translated by Philip Weyne (Baltimore: Penguin Books, 1965), p. 260.
33. Over the peaks calm,
    Scarcely a breath in the tree crowns,
    Silent the birds in the forest.
    Soon, you too,
    Will find peace.
34. Theodor W. Adorno, *Noten zur Literatur* (Frankfurt: Suhrkamp, 1958), pp. 80f.

35. Georg Büchner, *Sämtliche Werke und Briefe* (München: Carl Hanser, 1974), p. 87.

36. Adorno, *Noten zur Literatur* III, pp. 127, 126.

37. Horst Bredekamp, "Autonomie und Askese," in *Autonomie der Kunst,* pp. 121, 133.

38. Adorno, *Noten zur Literatur* III, p. 132.

39. Max Horkheimer and Theodor W. Adorno, *Dialectic of Enlightenment* (New York: Herder and Herder, 1972), p. 230 (translation corrected).

Bibliography

Books and Articles in Books or Periodicals

Adorno, Theodor W., *Noten sur Literatur* (Frankfurt: Surkamp, 1958).

Benjamin, Walter, "Der Autor als Produzent," in *Marxismus und Literatur,* vol. II, edited by Fritz J. Raddatz (Reinbek: Rowohlt, 1969).

Benjamin, Walter, "Fragment über Methodenfragen einer Marxistischen Literatur-Analyse," in *Kursbuch* 20 (Frankfurt: Suhrkamp, 1970).

Brecht, Bertolt, *Gesammelte Werke,* vols. VII and VIII (Frankfurt: Suhrkamp, 1967).

Bredekamp, Horst, "Autonomie und Askese," in *Autonomie der Kunst* (Frankfurt: Suhrkamp, 1972).

Fischer, Ernst, *Auf den Spuren der Wirklichkeit: sechs Essays* (Reinbek: Rowohlt, 1968).

Goethe, Johann Wolfgang, *Faust,* Part II, translated by Philip Weyne (Baltimore: Penguin Books, 1965).

Goldmann, Lucien, *Colloque international sur la sociologie de la littérature* (Brussels: Institute de la Sociologie, 1974).

Goldmann, Lucien, *Towards a Sociology of the Novel* (London: Tavistock Publisher, 1975).

Habermas, Jürgen, *Legitimation Crisis* (Boston: Beacon Press, 1975).

Horkheimer, Max, and Theodor W. Adorno, *Dialectic of Enlightenment* (New York: Herder and Herder, 1972).

Köhler, Erich, *Ideal und Wirklichkeit in der Höfischen Epik* (Tübingen: Niemeyer, 1956; second edition, 1970).

Lowenthal, Leo, *Literature and the Image of Man* (Boston: Beacon Press, 1957). Published in German as *Das Bild des Menschen in der Literatur* (Neuwied: Luchterhand, 1966).

Lukács, Georg, "Es geht um den Realismus," in *Marxismus und Literatur,* vol. II, edited by Fritz J. Raddatz (Reinbek: Rowohlt, 1969).

Marcuse, Herbert, *Counterrevolution and Revolt* (Boston: Beacon Press, 1972).

Marcuse, Herbert, *Negations* (Boston: Beacon Press, 1968).

Märten, Lu, *Die Linkskurve* III, 5 (Berlin: May 1931, reprinted 1970).

Nietzsche, Friedrich, *Der Wille zur Macht* (Stuttgart: Kroner, 1930).

Sander, Hans-Dietrich, *Marxistische Ideologie und allgemeine Kunsttheorie* (Tübingen: Mohr, 1970).

Sartre, Jean-Paul, *On a raison de se révolter* (Paris: Gallimard, 1974).

Index

High Middle Ages: 66–67
Historical materialism: 3
Hope, as categorical imperative in art: 57–58
Hubris, in art: 57–58
Hugo, Victor: 23
Humanity, pure: 58
The Humiliated and the Offended (Dostoyevsky): 23
Hundejahre (Grass): *xi*

Ibsen, Henrik: 48
Id: 43–44
Ideal, images of: 58
Ideology: 3
  art as, 1, 13
Illusion:
  art as, 48–49, 54
  a quality of reality, 56
Individual(s):
  concept of bourgeois, 38–39
  fate of, 24–26
  and goal of revolutions, 69
  subjectivity of, 3–5, 38
  unfreedom of, 71–72
The Introduction to the Critique of Political Economy (Marx): 15
Inwardness, derided: 38
Iphigenie (Goethe): 22, 47, 58

Kafka, Franz: *xii,* 46, 66

Labor, mental and manual separated: 28
The Lady from the Sea (Ibsen): 48
Language:
  of art, 22

mimesis by means of, 45
Lebenswelt, transcended by protagonists: 23
Lenin, Nikolai: 56
  rejects truth of art, 57
Lenz (Büchner): 66
Lessing, Gotthold: 26
Liberation, promise of:
  the Beautiful and, 65
  fractured by reality, 47–48
  limits of, 68–69
  a quality of aesthetic form, 46
Literature: *ix,* 11
  bourgeois, 37–38
  elitist, 19–21
  function of, 12
  mimesis in, 45
  revolutionary, *xii,* 73*n.*6
Logic, dialectical: 55
Luther, Martin: 67

Mallarmé, Stéphane: 19
Märtin, Lu: 12
Marx, Karl: 3, 11, 15, 16, 55, 74*n.*8
Marxism: *ix,* 17, 70
Material base, art and: 1, 3
Media, juxtaposition of: 50
Medieval epic, continued esteem for: 15
Mimesis:
  critical, 46
  in literature, 45
  memory and, 67
  renunciation of in anti-art, 50–51
  and transformation of reality, 44–45, 47–48, 63–64
  without transformation of reality, 51